AMERICAN HORTICULTURAL SOCIETY

WEEKLY PLANNER

Quarto.com

© 2026 Quarto Publishing Group USA Inc.

First Published in 2026 by Cool Springs Press, an imprint of The Quarto Group, 100 Cummings Center, Suite 265-D, Beverly, MA 01915, USA.
T (978) 282-9590 F (978) 283-2742

Cool Springs Press titles are also available at discount for retail, wholesale, promotional, and bulk purchase. For details, contact the Special Sales Manager by email at specialsales@quarto.com or by mail at The Quarto Group, Attn: Special Sales Manager, 100 Cummings Center, Suite 265-D, Beverly, MA 01915, USA.

30 29 28 27 26   1 2 3 4 5

ISBN: 978-1-57715-617-8

Design and Page Layout: Samantha J. Bednarek, samanthabednarek.com
Horticultural Reviewer: Botanist Scott Zona

Printed in Malaysia

Opposite page: *Lilium, Mary Vaux Walcott, 1925*

AMERICAN HORTICULTURAL SOCIETY

WEEKLY PLANNER

COOL SPRINGS PRESS

Thermopsis, Lupinus, Dalea, and Lathyrus, Edith S. Clements, 1920

MEET THE AMERICAN HORTICULTURAL SOCIETY

Founded in 1922, the nonprofit American Horticultural Society (AHS) is one of the most respected and longstanding member-based national gardening organizations in North America. The society's membership includes more than 22,000 aspiring, new, and experienced gardeners, plant enthusiasts, and horticultural professionals, as well as numerous regional and national partner organizations. Through its educational programs, awards, and publications, the AHS inspires a culture of gardening and horticultural practices that creates and sustains healthy, beautiful communities and a livable planet. AHS is headquartered at River Farm, a 27-acre (1 ha) site overlooking the Potomac River that is part of George Washington's original farmlands in Alexandria, Virginia. The AHS website is www.ahsgardening.org.

AMERICAN HORTICULTURAL SOCIETY

ABOUT THE ILLUSTRATIONS

The collected botanical illustrations in this book were created between the years 1774 and 1925 by their noted illustrators. The AHS would like to thank the Smithsonian Institution, the New York Botanical Garden, the Biodiversity Heritage Library, and the New York Public Library Digital Collections for their use. The book's front and back covers feature illustrations from Sydenham Edwards published in 1801. The endpaper illustrations were drawn by Edith S. Clements in 1920.

YEAR AT A GLANCE

January	February

May	June

September	October

March	April

July	August

November	December

Ratibida, Sydenham Edwards, 1801

YEAR	MONTH	WEEK
		○ ○ ○ ○ ○

_____ Monday

_____ Tuesday

_____ Wednesday

_____ Thursday

_____ Friday

_____ Saturday

_____ Sunday

YEAR

MONTH

WEEK

◯ ◯ ◯ ◯ ◯

_____ Monday

_____ Tuesday

_____ Wednesday

_____ Thursday

_____ Friday

_____ Saturday

_____ Sunday

Spigelia, Charles Frederick Millspaugh, 1887

Gentian, Sydenham Edwards, 1801

YEAR	MONTH	WEEK
		◯ ◯ ◯ ◯ ◯

_____ Monday

_____ Tuesday

_____ Wednesday

_____ Thursday

_____ Friday

_____ Saturday

_____ Sunday

YEAR	MONTH	WEEK
		◯ ◯ ◯ ◯ ◯

_____ Monday

_____ Tuesday

_____ Wednesday

_____ Thursday

_____ Friday

_____ Saturday

_____ Sunday

Asclepias, William Clark, 1826

Solidago, Mary Emily Eaton, 1916

_____ Monday

_____ Tuesday

_____ Wednesday

_____ Thursday

_____ Friday

_____ Saturday

_____ Sunday

_____ Monday

_____ Tuesday

_____ Wednesday

_____ Thursday

_____ Friday

_____ Saturday

_____ Sunday

Opuntia, Mary Emily Eaton, 1916

Helianthus, William Clark, 1826

_____ Monday

_____ Tuesday

_____ Wednesday

_____ Thursday

_____ Friday

_____ Saturday

_____ Sunday

_____ Monday

_____ Tuesday

_____ Wednesday

_____ Thursday

_____ Friday

_____ Saturday

_____ Sunday

Kalmia, Mary Emily Eaton, 1912

Cypripedium, Mary Emily Eaton, 1916

_____ Monday

_____ Tuesday

_____ Wednesday

_____ Thursday

_____ Friday

_____ Saturday

_____ Sunday

_____ Monday

_____ Tuesday

_____ Wednesday

_____ Thursday

_____ Friday

_____ Saturday

_____ Sunday

Echinacea, William Curtis, 1787

Magnolia, Pierre Joseph Redouté, 1801

_____ Monday

_____ Tuesday

_____ Wednesday

_____ Thursday

_____ Friday

_____ Saturday

_____ Sunday

_____ Monday

_____ Tuesday

_____ Wednesday

_____ Thursday

_____ Friday

_____ Saturday

_____ Sunday

Aloe, Nicolas-François Regnault, 1774

Allium, Sydenham Edwards, 1801

YEAR	MONTH	WEEK
		○ ○ ○ ○ ○

_____ Monday

_____ Tuesday

_____ Wednesday

_____ Thursday

_____ Friday

_____ Saturday

_____ Sunday

_____ Monday

_____ Tuesday

_____ Wednesday

_____ Thursday

_____ Friday

_____ Saturday

_____ Sunday

Mertensia, Mary Emily Eaton, 1916

Papaver (formerly Stylomecon), Matilda Smith, 1801

_____ Monday

_____ Tuesday

_____ Wednesday

_____ Thursday

_____ Friday

_____ Saturday

_____ Sunday

_____ Monday

_____ Tuesday

_____ Wednesday

_____ Thursday

_____ Friday

_____ Saturday

_____ Sunday

Echinopsis and Acanthocalycium, Mary Emily Eaton, 1916

Asarum, Jacob Bigelow, 1817

_____ Monday

_____ Tuesday

_____ Wednesday

_____ Thursday

_____ Friday

_____ Saturday

_____ Sunday

_____ Monday

_____ Tuesday

_____ Wednesday

_____ Thursday

_____ Friday

_____ Saturday

_____ Sunday

Symphyotrichum, Mary Emily Eaton, 1916

Juniperus, Pierre Joseph Redouté, 1801

_____ Monday

_____ Tuesday

_____ Wednesday

_____ Thursday

_____ Friday

_____ Saturday

_____ Sunday

YEAR	MONTH	WEEK
		◯ ◯ ◯ ◯ ◯

_____ Monday

_____ Tuesday

_____ Wednesday

_____ Thursday

_____ Friday

_____ Saturday

_____ Sunday

Polygonatum, Maurice Pillard Verneuil, 1896

Hydrangea, Pierre Joseph Redouté, 1801

○ ○ ○ ○ ○

_____ Monday

_____ Tuesday

_____ Wednesday

_____ Thursday

_____ Friday

_____ Saturday

_____ Sunday

YEAR	MONTH	WEEK
		◯ ◯ ◯ ◯ ◯

_____ Monday

_____ Tuesday

_____ Wednesday

_____ Thursday

_____ Friday

_____ Saturday

_____ Sunday

Rubus, Pierre Joseph Redouté, 1801

Sanguinaria, Issac Sprague, 1882

_____ Monday

_____ Tuesday

_____ Wednesday

_____ Thursday

_____ Friday

_____ Saturday

_____ Sunday

_____ Monday

_____ Tuesday

_____ Wednesday

_____ Thursday

_____ Friday

_____ Saturday

_____ Sunday

Phlox, Mary Vaux Walcott, 1925

Aronia, Mary Emily Eaton, 1916

YEAR	MONTH	WEEK
		○ ○ ○ ○ ○

_____ Monday

_____ Tuesday

_____ Wednesday

_____ Thursday

_____ Friday

_____ Saturday

_____ Sunday

_____ Monday

_____ Tuesday

_____ Wednesday

_____ Thursday

_____ Friday

_____ Saturday

_____ Sunday

Helianthus, Matilda Smith, 1801

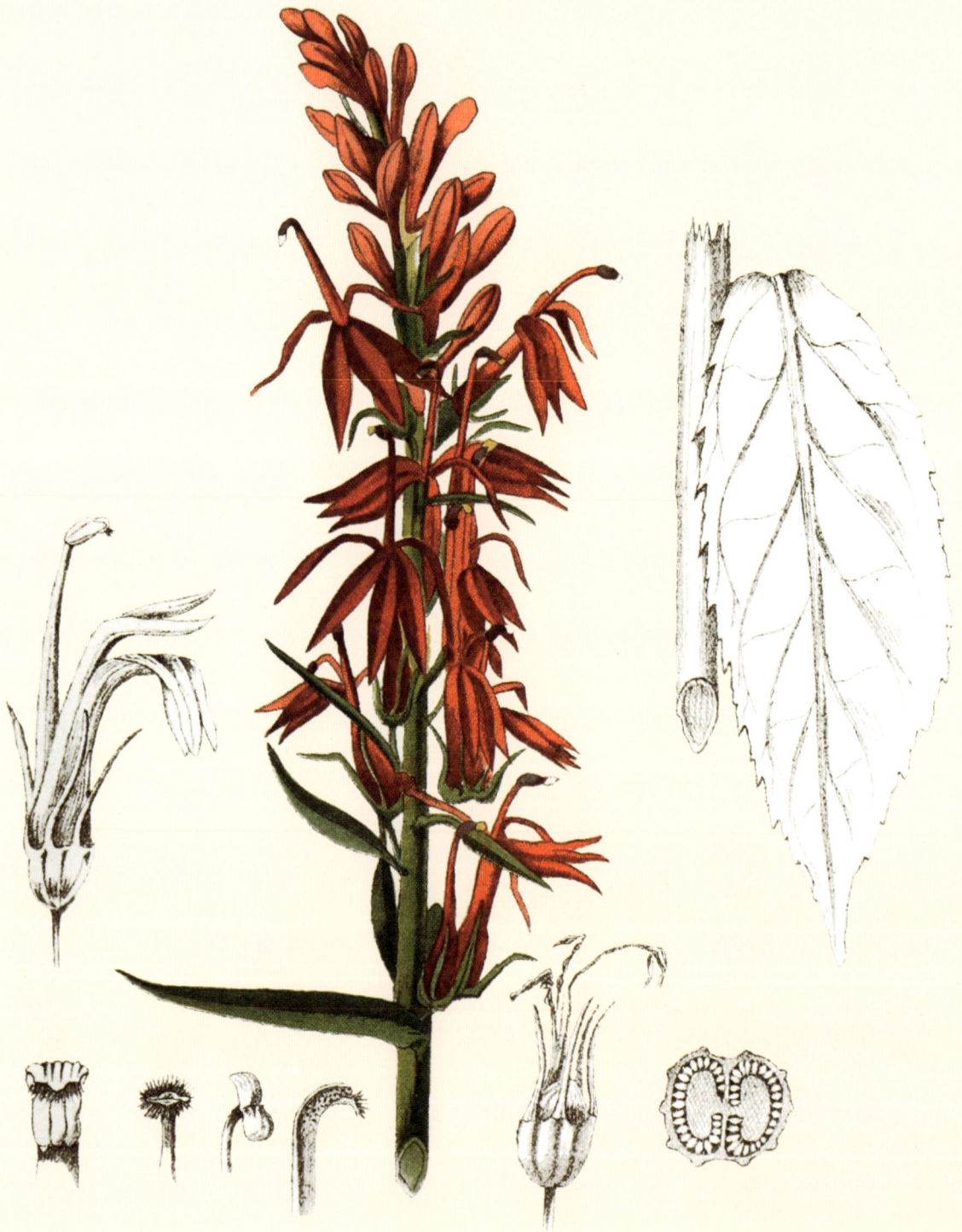

Lobelia, Charles Frederick Millspaugh, 1887

_____ Monday

_____ Tuesday

_____ Wednesday

_____ Thursday

_____ Friday

_____ Saturday

_____ Sunday

_____ Monday

_____ Tuesday

_____ Wednesday

_____ Thursday

_____ Friday

_____ Saturday

_____ Sunday

Sagittaria, Maurice Pillard Verneuil, 1896

Clematis, Mary Emily Eaton, 1916

_____ Monday

_____ Tuesday

_____ Wednesday

_____ Thursday

_____ Friday

_____ Saturday

_____ Sunday

_____ Monday

_____ Tuesday

_____ Wednesday

_____ Thursday

_____ Friday

_____ Saturday

_____ Sunday

Rhododendron, Pierre Joseph Redouté, 1801

Lyonia, Pierre Joseph Redouté, 1801

YEAR	MONTH	WEEK
		◯ ◯ ◯ ◯ ◯

_____ Monday

_____ Tuesday

_____ Wednesday

_____ Thursday

_____ Friday

_____ Saturday

_____ Sunday

_____ Monday

_____ Tuesday

_____ Wednesday

_____ Thursday

_____ Friday

_____ Saturday

_____ Sunday

Coreopsis, Mary Emily Eaton, 1916

Rhododendron, Pierre Joseph Redouté, 1801

_____ Monday

_____ Tuesday

_____ Wednesday

_____ Thursday

_____ Friday

_____ Saturday

_____ Sunday

_____ Monday

_____ Tuesday

_____ Wednesday

_____ Thursday

_____ Friday

_____ Saturday

_____ Sunday

Aristolochia, Pierre Joseph Redouté, 1801

Cornus, Mary Vaux Walcott, 1925

YEAR	MONTH	WEEK
		○ ○ ○ ○ ○

_____ Monday

_____ Tuesday

_____ Wednesday

_____ Thursday

_____ Friday

_____ Saturday

_____ Sunday

_____ Monday

_____ Tuesday

_____ Wednesday

_____ Thursday

_____ Friday

_____ Saturday

_____ Sunday

Sarracenia, Mary Vaux Walcott, 1925

Aquilegia, Nicolas-François Regnault, 1774

_____ Monday

_____ Tuesday

_____ Wednesday

_____ Thursday

_____ Friday

_____ Saturday

_____ Sunday

_____ Monday

_____ Tuesday

_____ Wednesday

_____ Thursday

_____ Friday

_____ Saturday

_____ Sunday

Aconitum, Maurice Pillard Verneuil, 1896

Baptisia, Edward Step, 1896

YEAR

MONTH

WEEK

◯ ◯ ◯ ◯ ◯

_____ Monday

_____ Tuesday

_____ Wednesday

_____ Thursday

_____ Friday

_____ Saturday

_____ Sunday

○ ○ ○ ○ ○

_____ Monday

_____ Tuesday

_____ Wednesday

_____ Thursday

_____ Friday

_____ Saturday

_____ Sunday

Cornus, Mary Emily Eaton, 1916

Hamamelis, Mary Emily Eaton, 1916

_____ Monday

_____ Tuesday

_____ Wednesday

_____ Thursday

_____ Friday

_____ Saturday

_____ Sunday

_____ Monday

_____ Tuesday

_____ Wednesday

_____ Thursday

_____ Friday

_____ Saturday

_____ Sunday

Clethra, Mary Emily Eaton, 1916

Penstemon, Mary Emily Eaton, 1916

YEAR	MONTH	WEEK
		○ ○ ○ ○ ○

_____ Monday

_____ Tuesday

_____ Wednesday

_____ Thursday

_____ Friday

_____ Saturday

_____ Sunday

○ ○ ○ ○ ○

_____ Monday

_____ Tuesday

_____ Wednesday

_____ Thursday

_____ Friday

_____ Saturday

_____ Sunday

Lupinus, Nicolas-François Regnault, 1774

Trillium, Sydenham Edwards, 1801

_____ Monday

_____ Tuesday

_____ Wednesday

_____ Thursday

_____ Friday

_____ Saturday

_____ Sunday

_____ Monday

_____ Tuesday

_____ Wednesday

_____ Thursday

_____ Friday

_____ Saturday

_____ Sunday

Delphinium, Matilda Smith, 1801

Asclepias, Nicolas-François Regnault, 1774.

_____ Monday

_____ Tuesday

_____ Wednesday

_____ Thursday

_____ Friday

_____ Saturday

_____ Sunday

YEAR	MONTH	WEEK ○ ○ ○ ○ ○

_____ Monday

_____ Tuesday

_____ Wednesday

_____ Thursday

_____ Friday

_____ Saturday

_____ Sunday

Hepatica, Mary Emily Eaton, 1916

Cercis, Mary Emily Eaton, 1916

YEAR	MONTH	WEEK
		◯ ◯ ◯ ◯ ◯

_____ Monday

_____ Tuesday

_____ Wednesday

_____ Thursday

_____ Friday

_____ Saturday

_____ Sunday

_____ Monday

_____ Tuesday

_____ Wednesday

_____ Thursday

_____ Friday

_____ Saturday

_____ Sunday

Dicentra, Mary Vaux Walcott, 1925

Geranium, William Barton, 1818

YEAR	MONTH	WEEK
		○ ○ ○ ○ ○

_____ Monday

_____ Tuesday

_____ Wednesday

_____ Thursday

_____ Friday

_____ Saturday

_____ Sunday

_____ Monday

_____ Tuesday

_____ Wednesday

_____ Thursday

_____ Friday

_____ Saturday

_____ Sunday

Passiflora, Pierre Joseph Redouté, 1801

USEFUL INFORMATION